Monster Science

VAMPIRES AND LIGHT

BY JODY JENSEN SHAFFER • ILLUSTRATED BY GERVASIO

Consultant:
Joanne K. Olson, PhD
Associate Professor, Science Education
Iowa State University
Ames, Iowa

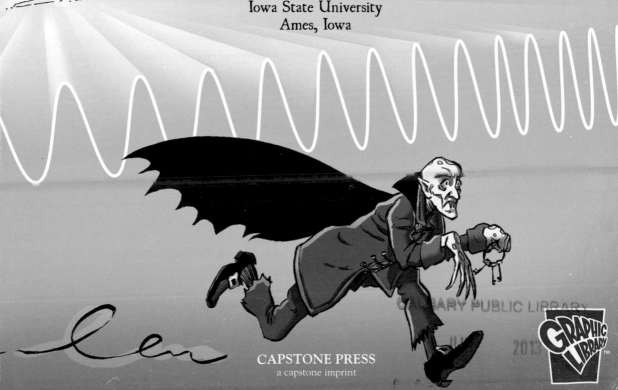

CAPSTONE PRESS
a capstone imprint

GRAPHIC LIBRARY

Graphic Library is published by Capstone Press,
1710 Roe Crest Drive, North Mankato, Minnesota 56003
www.capstonepub.com

Library of Congress Cataloging-in-Publication Data
Shaffer, Jody Jensen.
  Vampires and light / by Jody Jensen Shaffer ; illustrated by Gervasio.
    pages cm.—(Graphic library. Monster science)
  Summary: "In cartoon format, uses vampires to explain the science of light"—Provided
by publisher.
  Includes bibliographical references and index.
  ISBN 978-1-4296-9928-0 (library binding)
  ISBN 978-1-62065-820-8 (paperback)
  ISBN 978-1-4765-1592-2 (eBook PDF)
1. Light—Juvenile literature. 2. Light sources—Juvenile literature. 3. Optics—Juvenile literature. I.
Gervasio, illustrator. II. Title.
  QC360.S53 2013
  535—dc23   2012026436

Editor
Christopher L. Harbo

Designer
Alison Thiele

Art Director
Nathan Gassman

Production Specialist
Laura Manthe

For my dad, Dr. Gary Jensen, who gave me his love of science, language, and humor. And for my
mom, Evelyn Stoddard Jensen, for her curiosity, playfulness, and glass always half full. –JJS

Printed in the United States of America in Brainerd, Minnesota.
92012   006938BANGS13

TABLE OF
CONTENTS

CHAPTER 1

LIGHT IS ENERGY

Look around. The world is full of light. It brightens and warms our days.

UGH. WAKE ME WHEN IT'S DARK.

And we wouldn't see a thing without it.

NOW THIS IS MORE LIKE IT!

But what is light?

I DON'T WANT TO KNOW.

SIZZZZLE!

All things are either matter or energy. Matter includes objects, such as solids, liquids, and gases. Energy is not an object. It is the ability to do work. Light is one form of energy.

HEE HEE!

AHHHHH!

In simple terms, energy makes things move and change.

It also helps animals and plants grow. In fact, light energy makes all life on Earth possible.

... OR MORE DIFFICULT.

You don't have to look far to see many sources of light. Some are natural, such as stars.

OOooooOO.

Others are made by people, such as the bulbs in Flashlights. Lightbulbs change electricity into light energy.

Here on Earth no source of light is greater than the sun.

FSSSSSSSS

DO I SMELL SOMETHING BURNING?

The energy it streams to our planet is the key to our very existence.

Without sunlight, we wouldn't have day and night or the changing seasons.

I'M A VAMPIRE FOR ALL SEASONS.

Sunlight also gives plants the energy they need to perform photosynthesis. This process allows them to make the food they need to live and grow.

photosynthesis—process by which plants make food using sunlight, carbon dioxide, and water

Without sunlight, plants would wither and die.

Not so fast. Without plants, people and animals that depend on them for food would also die. All life on Earth would vanish.

CHAPTER 2

HOW LIGHT WORKS

We know light is important to life, but how is it created? Under special conditions, light can be created in atoms. These tiny particles are the building blocks of matter.

BLOOD BANK

ATOM

atom—smallest particle of an element

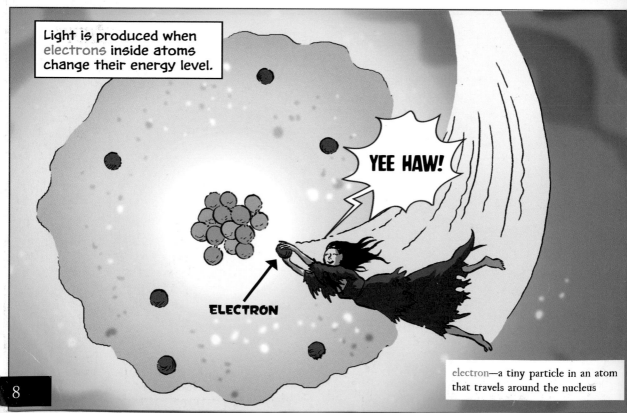

Light is produced when electrons inside atoms change their energy level.

YEE HAW!

ELECTRON

electron—a tiny particle in an atom that travels around the nucleus

Atoms produce light that travels in waves, much like the waves on the ocean.

Light waves are measured in wavelengths. A wavelength is the distance between the tops of two waves.

WAVELENGTH

Some wavelengths are short. They move more quickly and for shorter distances than long wavelengths.

WAHOO!

Long wavelengths move slowly and have less energy.

Energy that comes from the sun includes a range of long and short wavelengths. Together these wavelengths make up the electromagnetic spectrum.

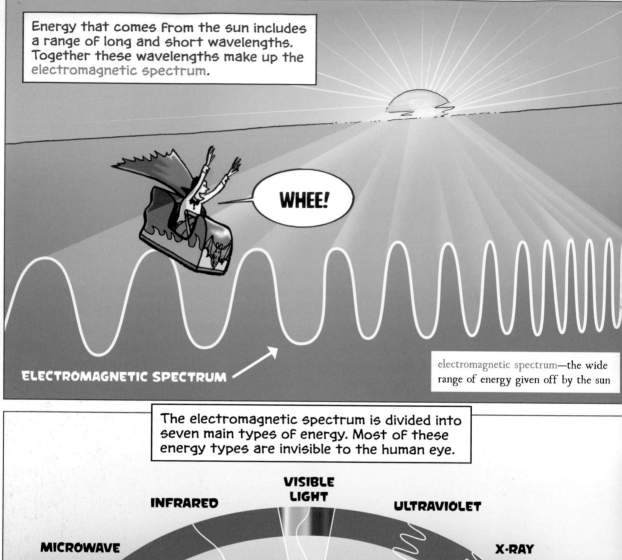

WHEE!

ELECTROMAGNETIC SPECTRUM →

electromagnetic spectrum—the wide range of energy given off by the sun

The electromagnetic spectrum is divided into seven main types of energy. Most of these energy types are invisible to the human eye.

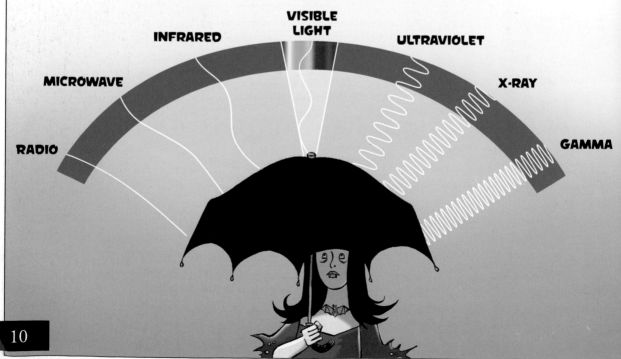

VISIBLE LIGHT

INFRARED

ULTRAVIOLET

MICROWAVE

X-RAY

RADIO

GAMMA

Long, low-energy wavelengths make up one end of the electromagnetic spectrum. Although you can't see radio waves and microwaves, you use them every day.

Infrared light is another long, low-energy wavelength you can't normally see. But with night-vision goggles, you can see how all things that produce heat also give off infrared light.

I'LL NEVER GO HUNGRY WITH THESE GOGGLES!

On the other end of the electromagnetic spectrum are the invisible short wavelengths. Unless you use sunscreen, the sun's ultraviolet light can cause sunburns.

I'M NOT TAKING ANY CHANCES.

Doctors use high-energy X-rays to find broken bones. They use gamma rays to kill cancer cells.

I SEE A WOODEN STAKE AND TWO SILVER BULLETS.

I'VE HAD A ROUGH DAY.

We can't see the energy on either end of the electromagnetic spectrum. But we can see the energy between these extremes.

COLORS OR NO COLORS, I'M OUT OF HERE!

The visible light spectrum includes white light and the colors hidden within it.

How did we learn about white light's secrets?

ISAAC NEWTON

In the 1600s, scientist Sir Isaac Newton figured out that white light is actually made of many colors.

People knew that when light shined through a prism, a rainbow could be created. What they didn't know was what made the colors.

Was it something special inside the glass, or were the colors a part of the light itself?

WHOA! WATCH WHERE YOU'RE AIMING THAT THING!

prism—a transparent, triangle-shaped plastic or glass object that bends light

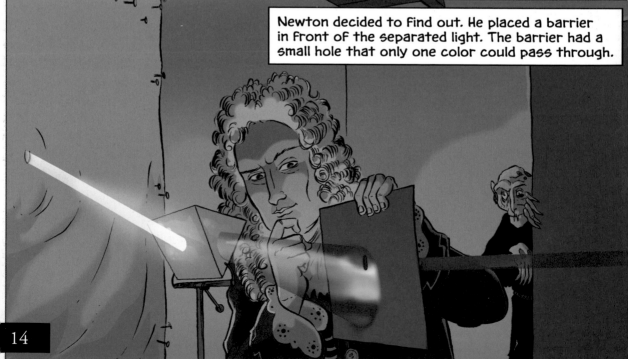

Newton decided to find out. He placed a barrier in front of the separated light. The barrier had a small hole that only one color could pass through.

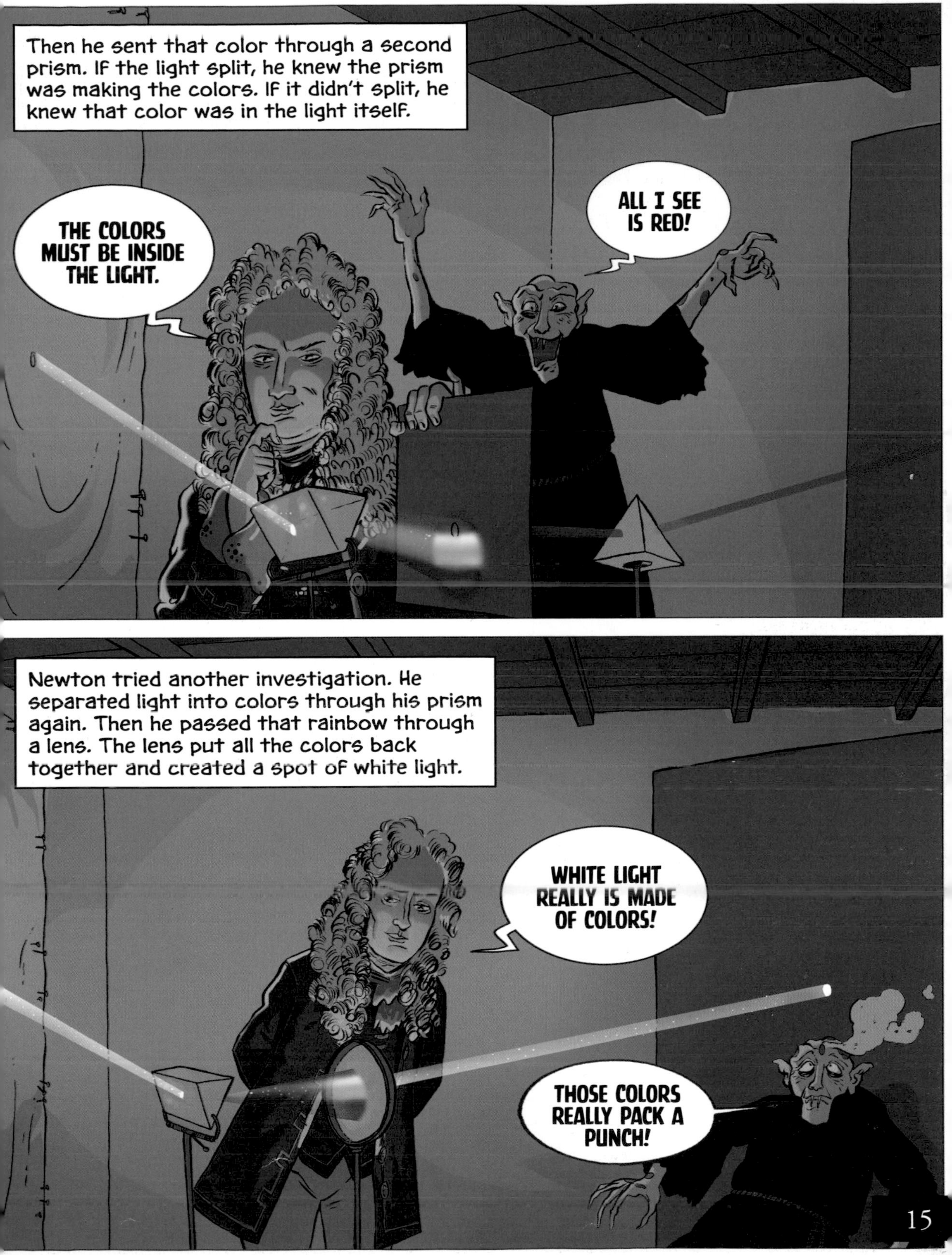

Then he sent that color through a second prism. If the light split, he knew the prism was making the colors. If it didn't split, he knew that color was in the light itself.
THE COLORS MUST BE INSIDE THE LIGHT.
ALL I SEE IS RED!
Newton tried another investigation. He separated light into colors through his prism again. Then he passed that rainbow through a lens. The lens put all the colors back together and created a spot of white light.
WHITE LIGHT REALLY IS MADE OF COLORS!
THOSE COLORS REALLY PACK A PUNCH!

You don't need a glass prism to see Newton's investigation in action. When you look at a rainbow, you're seeing the sun's white light split into colors.

DON'T WASTE YOUR TIME, LASSIE.

BIP BIP BIP

Rainbows form when light passes through water droplets in the air. The water droplets act like tiny prisms. They split sunlight into bands of red, orange, yellow, green, blue, indigo, and violet.

EEEEKKK!

The order of colors in rainbows never changes. Red has the longest wavelength. Violet had the shortest.

I LOVE RED!

To remember the order of wavelengths between red and violet, just think about the simple phrase ROY G. BIV.

BWA HAHA HAHA!

LASER LIGHT

Lasers concentrate light onto a tiny point by producing light waves with the same wavelength. That single wavelength can pack a lot of power. Some lasers are powerful enough to melt metal, cut diamonds, or perform surgery.

CHAPTER 3

CHARACTERISTICS OF LIGHT

Besides its wavelengths, scientists have studied many other characteristics of light. One of the most amazing is its speed.

I NEED SPEED!

Light travels at about 186,000 miles (299,300 kilometers) per second. Scientists call this the speed of light.

Light is faster than anything else in the universe. It travels 93 million miles (150 million km) from the sun to the Earth in about eight minutes.

UGH. RIGHT ON TIME ... AGAIN!

Light is so fast, a single beam could travel to the moon and back in less than three seconds!

OW!

To see the speed of light in action, look no further than a thunderstorm. Because light travels much faster than sound, you see a lightning bolt before you hear thunder.

After seeing a lightning bolt, slowly count 1,000, 2,000, 3,000, until you hear thunder. Every five seconds you count equals about 1 mile (1.6 km). If you hear thunder after 10 seconds, you know that lightning struck about 2 miles (3.2 km) away.

... 8,000, 9,000, 10,000 ...

BOOM!

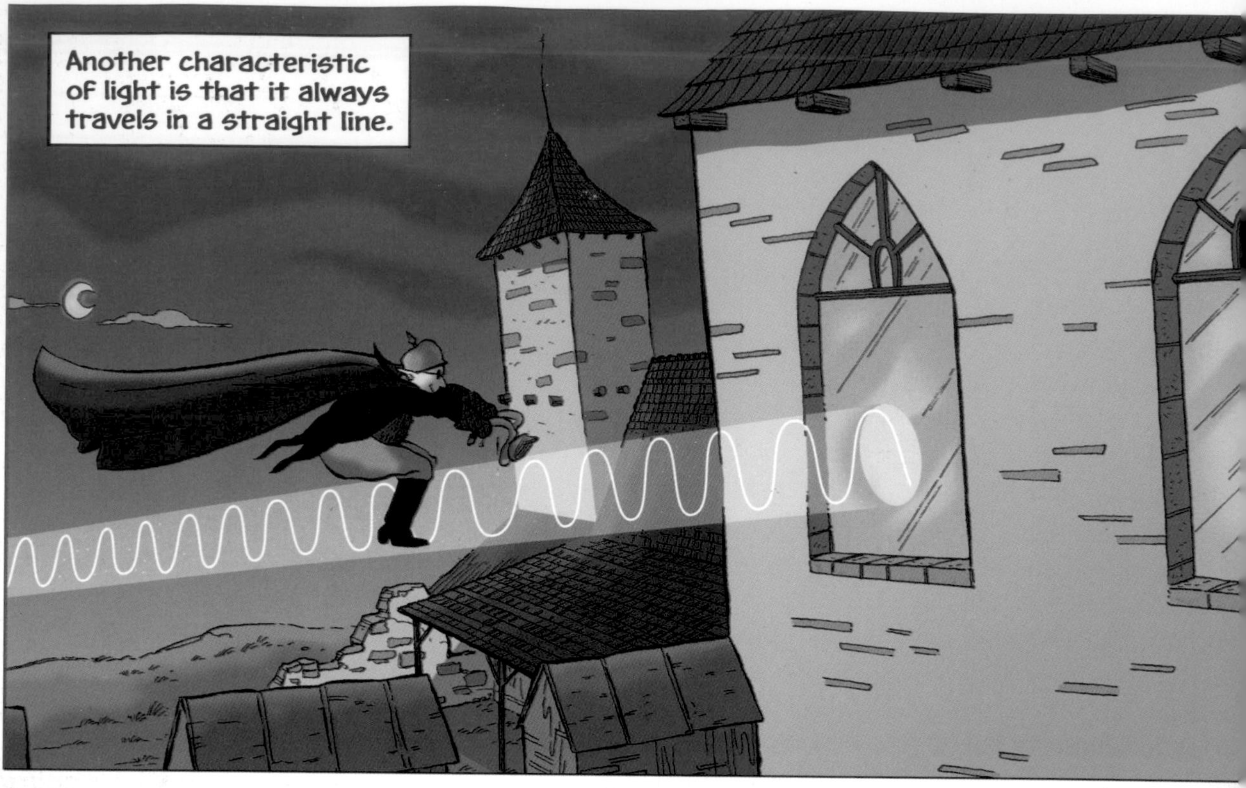

Another characteristic of light is that it always travels in a straight line.

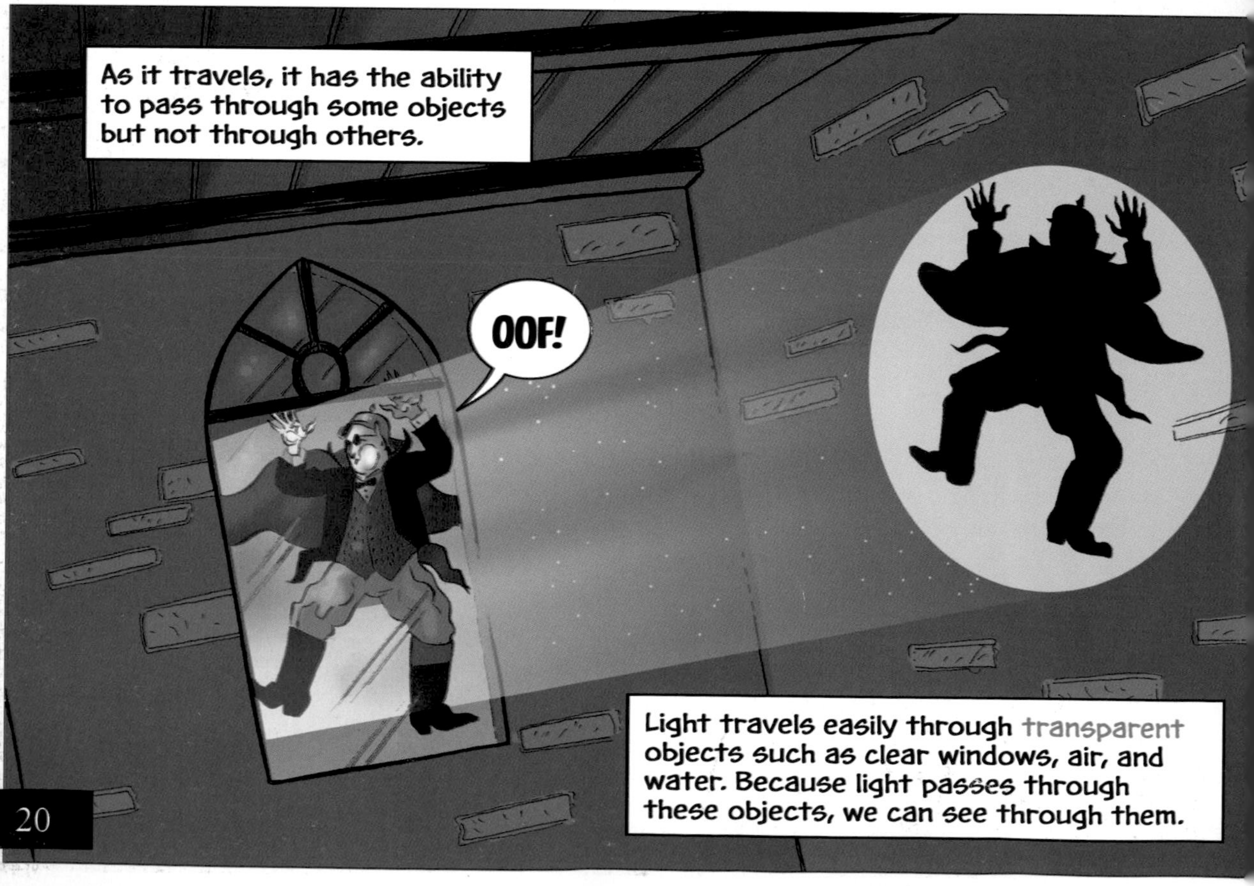

As it travels, it has the ability to pass through some objects but not through others.
OOF!
Light travels easily through transparent objects such as clear windows, air, and water. Because light passes through these objects, we can see through them.

Light also passes through objects such as clouds, fabric, and stained glass. But these objects are translucent. They let some light through, but not all of it. We can't see through these objects to the other side.

SIZZZZLE!

BAH! I NEED A THICKER CLOAK!

Of course, many objects don't let any light through at all. These objects are opaque. When light hits opaque objects, a dark spot, or shadow, forms behind them.

transparent—letting light pass through
translucent—letting light pass through, but not transparent
opaque—blocking light

Most objects do not produce light. To see something, light has to come from a source, such as the sun or a lightbulb.

The light then hits an object. After hitting the object, the light reflects into your eyes. The way light is reflected or absorbed by objects affects what they look like.

Smooth, light-colored objects reflect light well. For instance, the moon does not produce light. You see the moon because sunlight reflects off its gray surface and streams to Earth.

AAAAOOOOO!

HEY, THAT'S MY LINE!

Shiny objects are especially good at reflecting light. You see your image in a mirror because the light from the lightbulb bounces off your body. The light from your body travels to the mirror. Then it reflects off the mirror and into your eyes.

UNLESS YOU'RE A VAMPIRE!

reflect—to return light from an object
absorb—to soak light up

22

Rough, dark objects reflect light poorly. Things like brown bats and black capes reflect little or no light. Instead they absorb much of the light that hits them.

How an object reflects or absorbs light also determines the colors you see. When light hits an object, only the color of that object reflects back to you. The object absorbs all the other colors.

A red apple reflects the color red. A green leaf reflects green. A black cape absorbs all the colors, and a white handkerchief reflects them.

STAYING COOL

Color has a lot to do with heat too. Stand outside on a sunny day. You'll feel how the sun produces both light and heat. But did you know that the color of your clothes can change how hot or cool you feel? Light colors like white and yellow reflect a lot of light and heat. Dark blue and black absorb much of the light and heat. If you want to stay cool on a sunny day, wear the lightest color clothing you can find.

NOW YOU TELL ME.

SIZZZZLE!

BUS STOP

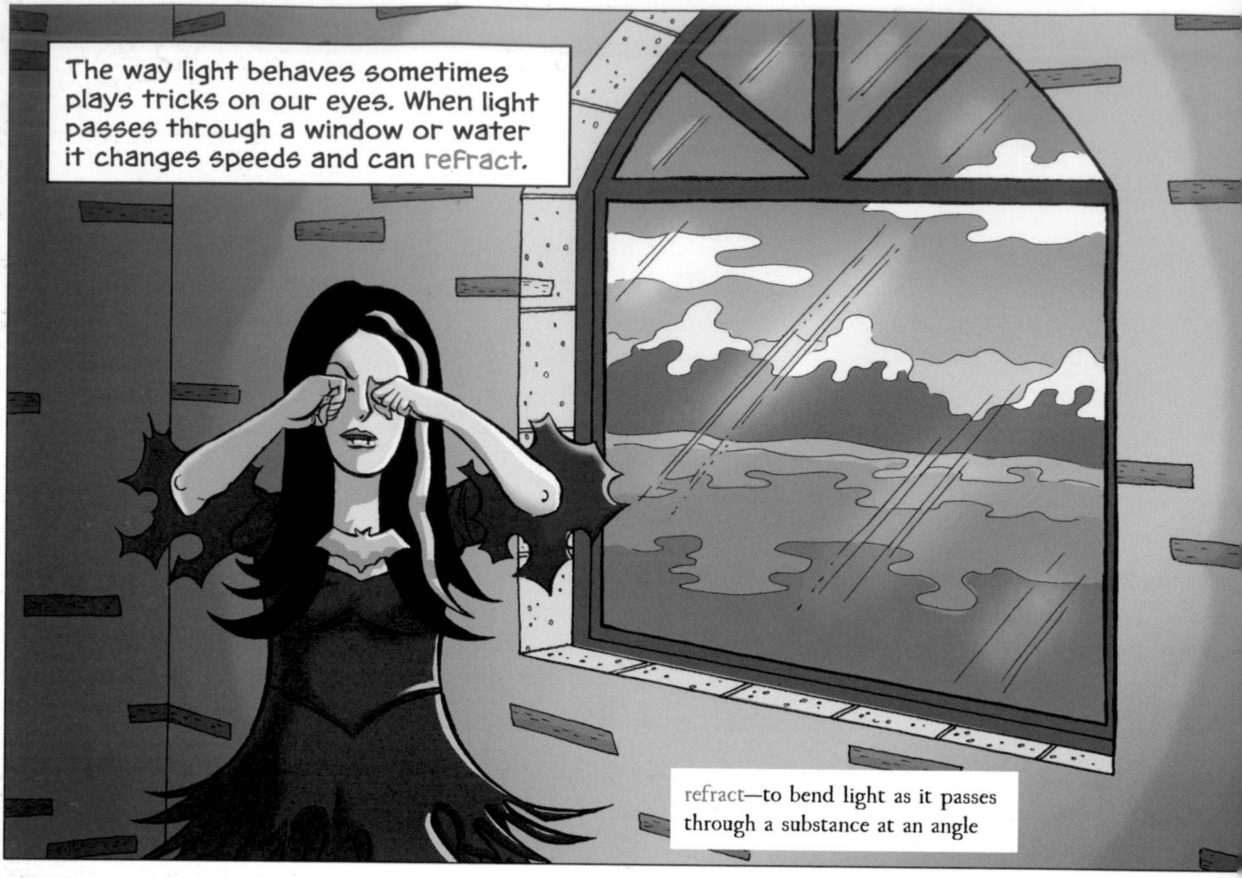
The way light behaves sometimes plays tricks on our eyes. When light passes through a window or water it changes speeds and can refract.

refract—to bend light as it passes through a substance at an angle

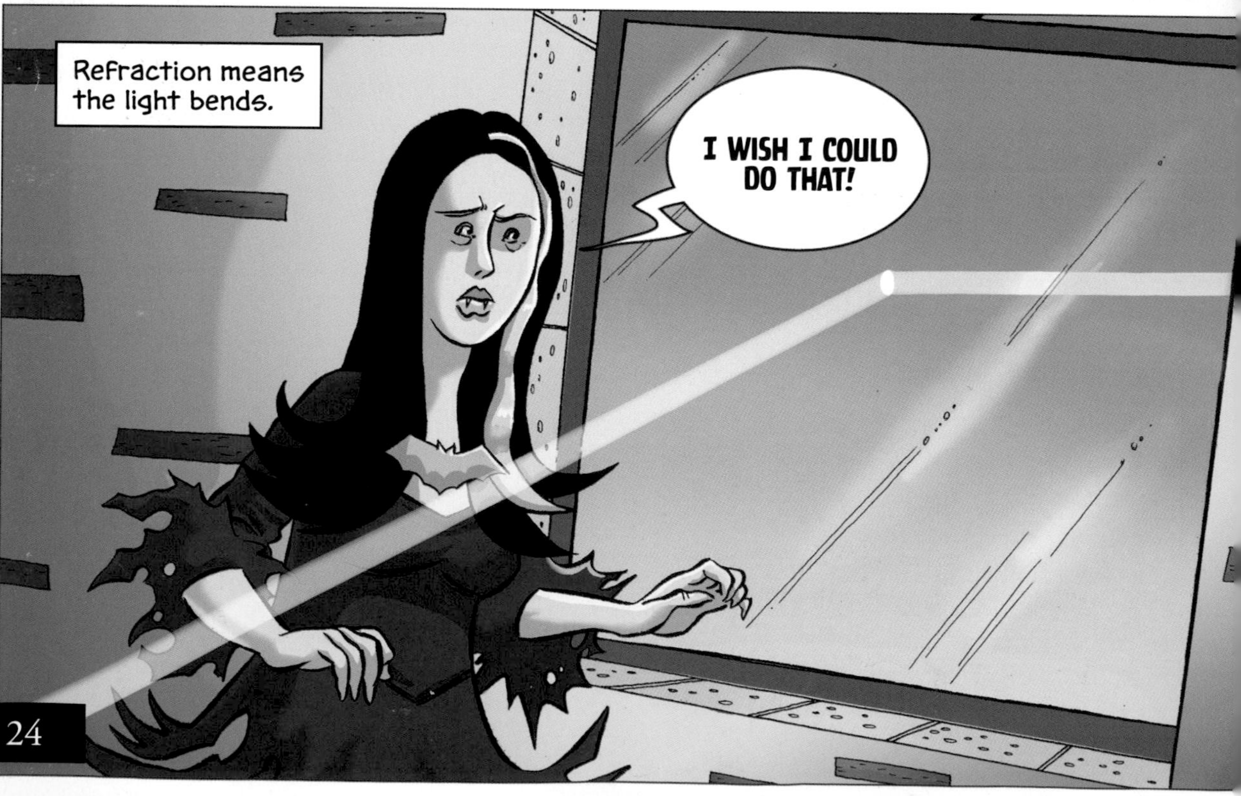
Refraction means the light bends.
I WISH I COULD DO THAT!

When light changes speeds and bends, objects don't always look normal. For instance, a straw in a glass of water looks broken.

STRAWS ARE TRICKY FOR VAMPIRES.

We see the straw because light reflects off it and into our eyes. But the light coming from the bottom part of the straw passes through both water and glass. The two materials bend the light so much the straw looks broken.

You can also see refraction at work when you look down into a fishbowl. The water refracts the light. Objects on the bottom look closer than they really are.

YIKES!

CHAPTER 4

LIGHT FOR LIFE

Light can do amazing things, but it's what we do with it that really impacts our lives. The biggest way you use light every day is with your eyes.

Your eyes are powerful. When light reflects off an object, it enters your eye through the cornea and then the pupil.

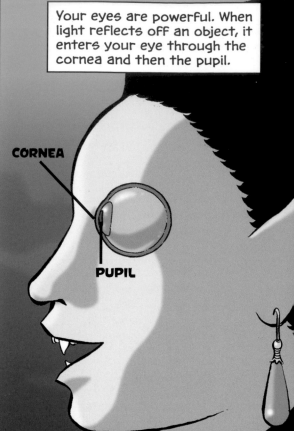

CORNEA

PUPIL

Light then passes through the eye's lens. The lens bends the light and focuses it upside down on the retina at the back of the eye.

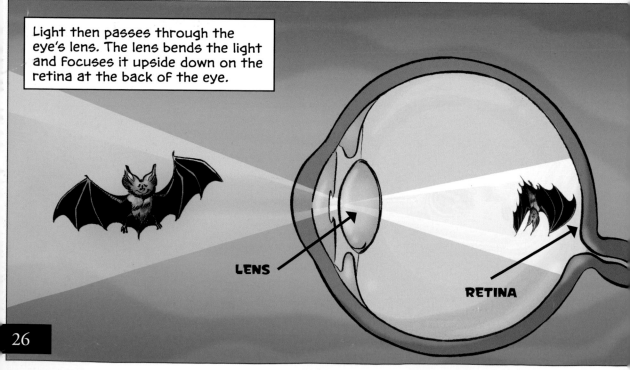

LENS

RETINA

The retina has cells called rods and cones that detect light. Rods sense light and dark, shapes, and movement. Cones sense colors and details.

The optic nerve carries signals about what you see from the eye to your brain. Your brain flips over the images it receives so you see everything right side up.

Every day, light plays an important role in our lives. We need light to see, work, and play.

Without light we'd be in total darkness. We wouldn't be able to see anything.

WHAT'S WRONG WITH THAT?

We need light for energy. Plants depend on sunlight for their food. We depend on plants, and the animals that eat them, for ours.

I PREFER A LIQUID DIET.

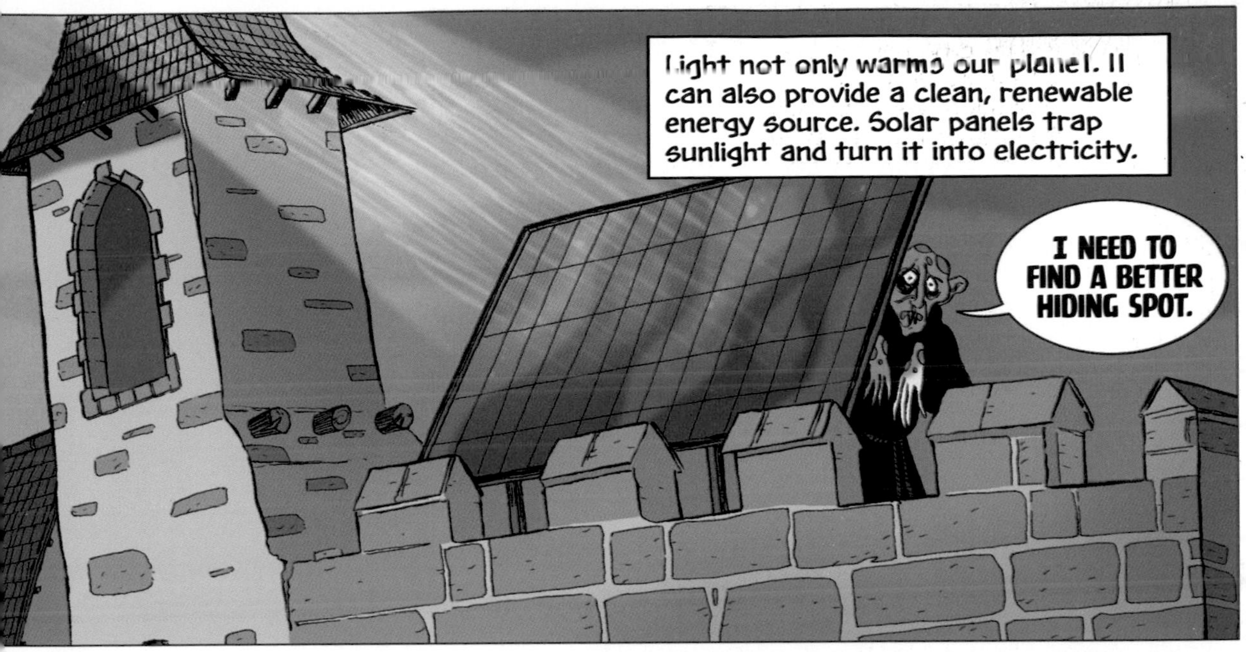
Light not only warms our planet. It can also provide a clean, renewable energy source. Solar panels trap sunlight and turn it into electricity.
I NEED TO FIND A BETTER HIDING SPOT.

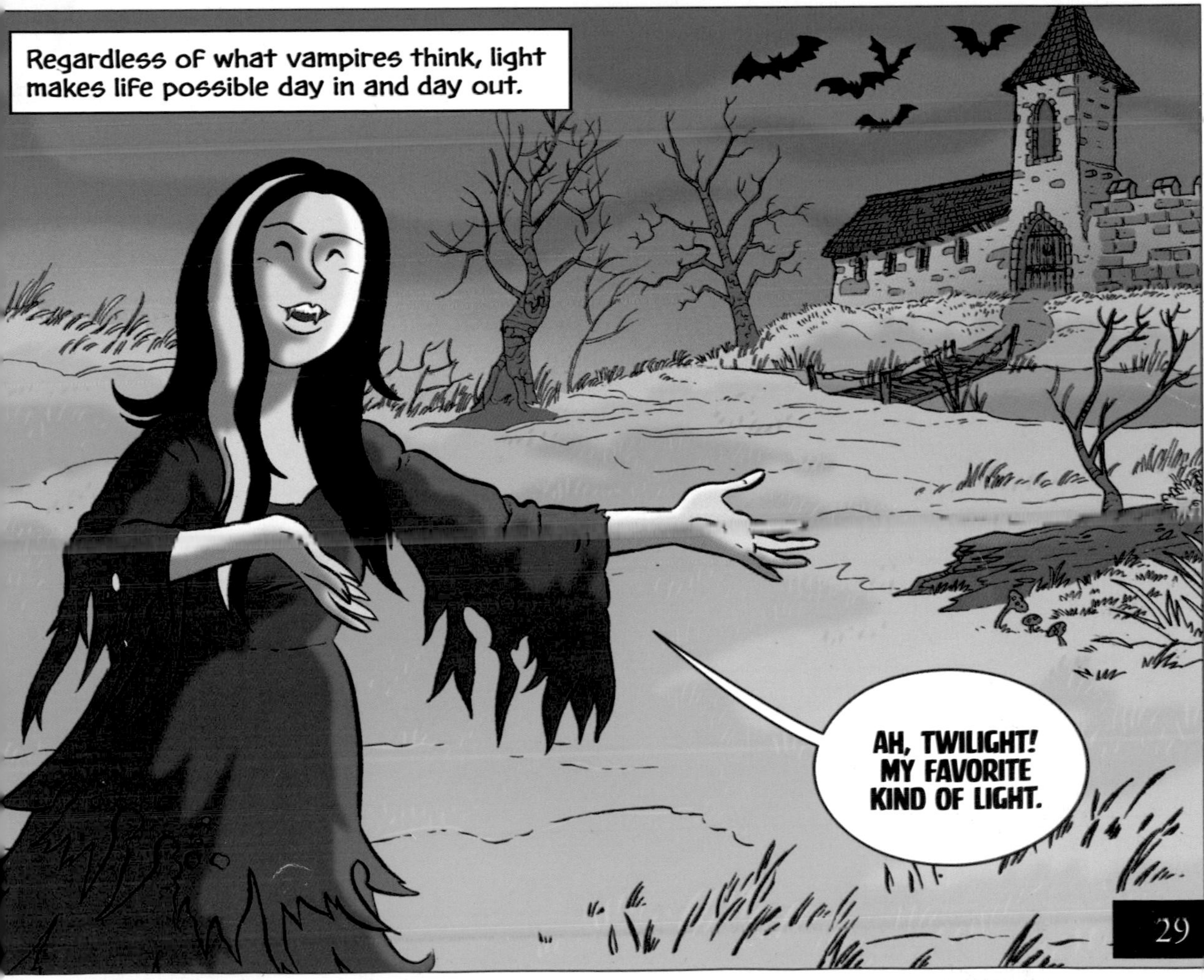
Regardless of what vampires think, light makes life possible day in and day out.
AH, TWILIGHT! MY FAVORITE KIND OF LIGHT.

GLOSSARY

absorb (ab-ZORB)—to soak up light

atom (AT-uhm)—smallest particle of an element

electromagnetic spectrum (i-lek-troh-mag-NET-ic SPEK-truhm)—the wide range of energy given off by the sun

electron (i-LEK-tron)—a tiny particle in an atom that travels around the nucleus

energy (EN-ur-jee)—the ability to do work, such as moving things or giving heat or light

matter (MAT-ur)—anything that has weight and takes up space

opaque (oh-PAKE)—blocking light

photosynthesis (foh-toh-SIN-thuh-siss)—process by which plants make food using sunlight, carbon dioxide, and water

prism (PRIZ-uhm)—a transparent, triangle-shaped plastic or glass object that bends light

reflect (ri-FLEKT)—to return light from an object

refract (ri-FRAKT)—to bend light as it passes through a substance at an angle

translucent (trans-LOO-suhnt)—letting light pass through, but not transparent; frosted and stained glass are translucent

transparent (transs-PAIR-uhnt)—letting light pass through

wavelength (WAYV-length)—the distance between two peaks of a wave

READ MORE

Claybourne, Anna. *Secrets of Light.* Science Secrets. New York: Marshall Cavendish Benchmark, 2011.

Nunn, Daniel. *Shadows and Reflections.* Light All around Us. Chicago: Heinemann Library, 2013.

Walker, Sally M. *Investigating Light.* How Does Energy Work? Minneapolis: Lerner Publications, 2012.

Whiting, Jim. *Light.* Mysteries of the Universe. Mankato, Minn.: Creative Education, 2012.

Woodford, Chris. *Light: Investigating Visible and Invisible Electromagnetic Radiation.* Scientific Pathways. New York: Rosen Central, 2013.

INTERNET SITES

FactHound offers a safe, fun way to find Internet sites related to this book. All sites on FactHound have been researched by our staff.

Here's all you do:

Visit *www.facthound.com*

Type in this code: 9781429699280

Check out projects, games and lots more at
www.capstonekids.com

INDEX